1

Sergio Barone

●

PROMOTIONAL IDEAS

FOR YOUR BAR OR NIGHT CLUB

By Sergio Barone

Sergio Barone

Sun Media Group LLC · 1st Edition · Printed in the United States of America

●

PROMOTIONAL IDEAS

FOR YOUR BAR OR NIGHT CLUB

INTRODUCTION

If you're an owner or thinking of becoming an owner or promoter of a bar or night club your success will be determined upon your knowledge in the bar and entertainment business. You are in a business where the cash rewards are great and the risk of capital loss even greater. We will briefly review some aspects of a bar and night club. We hope you will find this information helpful to you. In the long run, your own decisions will determine all your successes or failures.

CONCEPT, NAME, NIGHT CLUB LOCATION

What is Concept?...An idea conceived in the mind.

Starting a "Bar" or "Night Club" requires you to have an idea of what you plan to achieve. You have to decide what kind of establishment you want. There are a lot of variables.. Examples: What type of venue do you intend to be labeled as? "Bar, Dance Club, Rock Club, Teen Club, Alternative Club, Event Club, Rave Club, Go-Go Bar, Sports Club, Tavern?" Do you have an idea what type of crowd that might attend? Younger, older audiences? Do you intend to promote different events for each day, different music each day? Plan your strategy. In some instances, the sound decibels of the music should be taken into consideration to promote either a relaxing atmosphere or a loud high energy sound. A clubs most successful life is approximately 2 years. There have been a few instances where they have lasted 20 years or more with the same name.

5

SELECTING A BUSINESS NAME?

At this very moment you've always had at least one name for your club in mind. Surprisingly to me as it is, a name does matter. There have been names that have caught on very well, in which I feel have definitely contributed to the success of a club. There are no rights or wrongs in a name unless proven otherwise. Some names are more easy to remember than others. When deciding on a name, keep in mind how it would sound to others. How would it sound on the radio? How would it look in advertising, promotional materials? Do you think it can hold up in the future without sounding outdated? Overall, do you think it would work? Use your judgment. If you think you need opinions, ask for them. You can always change the name easily before you actually decide to use it. Sketch some type of logo which instantaneously represents your club at a glance. Incorporate a design with the name or slogan. Do not get over complicated with your art. Do not get too complicated with typefaces. People do not want to spend a lot of time trying to figure out what your trying to say. After you decide on your business name(s), file forms with your city to register your name choice. It may or may not already be taken.

LOCATION

If you have yet to open a bar or club select a city or location which will understand your plans and will work with you in achieving your goals. Do not attempt anything at grand scale unless the city is in full agreement with what you plan to do. Go talk to city officials and board members. A very important factor to consider is to choose a location in which the ordinances will let you stay open as late as possible. You don't want to lose customers because you have to close your doors too early.

Never start constructing, designing, remodeling any new facility without thoroughly investigating city ordinances. There have been instances where projects under construction have been cancelled due to not following procedures and meeting zoning restrictions. Consult your insurance agent on the necessary coverage for liability and for the use of alcohol on the premises.

When you open for business, and you have promoted successfully, you will find that everyone will come to see the in thing, "Your Establishment." The critical part will now begin. Offering the public something that will make them choose your place over someone elses in the future. That's called, "Successful Promotions."

Some criteria for choosing a location:

1) Select an area with low percentage of surrounding nightly entertainment establishments.

2) Well kept area of the city.

3) Easily accessibility to your location through main streets and major highways.

4) Plenty of parking or side street parking.

5) Good police and security departments.

6) An area not in a so desolate area, but not too close to residential.

NIGHT CLUB EXTERIOR

In art as an expressionistic form, we as humans are attracted first and foremost to form, rather than color. Determine if your night club is architecturally attractive. Secondly, color is a factor in determining pleasant surroundings and having people feel you have a secure, well liked, up to the times bar or club.

Though such aesthetic factors are important in reaching a certain clientele, it does not always apply, such in cases where cities are limited to space and buildings are close together. These night clubs would make their design value in the interior.

If you are considering exterior renovations, always experiment on paper what effects you would like to achieve. Always ask for opinions to whom you feel may be qualified to give you advice. You do not have to follow it, but not asking for it can cost you money in oversights.

Sergio Barone

Remedies for improving your exterior may only require paint, filling in cracks, holes, etc. Do renovations yourself, with a friend or hire a reasonable contractor. If you are not sure about the direction of the looks you are planning to achieve, contact a decorating or architectural firm for advise. Research books about signage and architecture. It would make sense to spend some money than to make costly mistakes.

Renovate as your budget allow. Achieve a look of the clientele you plan to attract. Whether it be a young 21 to 35 age group, 35 and over age group, upscale clientele, middle-class clientele, young adult clientele, you can achieve the results with exterior renovations. Again, experiment on paper.

NIGHT CLUB INTERIOR
How should the interior look? Who should design it? What audio equipment should I use for sound? Should you hire artists to paint murals? Your interior should somewhat reflect the clientele you intend to attract. Your club should also contain some sort of atmosphere you intent to portray. Do you intend to have your club dim or brightly lit. There are various types of lighting schemes available. Neon usually works very well because of its attractiveness and the ability to shape it in many ways. There are various materials and ideas you can choose which will give you the effect your looking for. Your interior will make a statement, in which you and possibly your architect or interior designer will have developed. Always ask for different designer's opinions who you feel are qualified to help.

One thing that cannot be stressed enough is sound. Your club will be as good as you sound. If you can purchase low cost equipment and make the music sound terrific, that's great. On the other hand, if you have no experience of sound techniques, don't hesitate to call a sound technician for advice. He will recommend and install what will work. Do not listen to someone you have the slightest doubt about, this would probably be a person who does not make a living as a sound tech. Your sound has to be clear and

8

able to sustain high power with minimum distortion. Your system has to be equipped with the necessary audio equipment which can provide a disc jockey with what he needs. Your system should also include equipment in which a performer will also need to use such as; microphones, turn-tables, cd's or other requirements. Any equipment that you intend to use must at all times be kept functional.

Should you use a stage? Stages can be rented if you don't plan to install one. If you intend to hire bands, track acts or other performing artist's regularly it would make sense to install one or more stages.

There are small dance floors, large dance floors, multilevel dance floors, and no dance floors. So what are the rights and wrongs of dance floors? Usually, when you spot numerous lights on the ceiling, that indicates the dance floor below. If you are looking to add a light show to your club then you might need some dance floor area. Go to area night clubs and evaluate their dance floor size and the amount of people they draw. Another idea could be to use a balance of space in your facility. Split equal amounts of the dance floor, bar(s), and interior. This criteria remains with the designer's intentions.

ABOUT ALCOHOLIC BEVERAGES

Almost all bars and related night clubs serve alcoholic beverages. Without alcohol and only serving juices and soda, these establishments would be categorized as juice bars. The restrictions of what you can do with live entertainment would vary. Anyone considering opening a bar business should contact their local Alcohol & Beverage Commission (ABC) and request their manual on regulations. In most cases, you will find them very willing to help with all your questions. You must have an alcohol beverage license to serve alcohol.

Alcoholic beverages supply the major income in a night club business. Their second source of income would be from general door admission. Then other income would be derived from food, V.I.P's, clothing and merchandising.

What is the connection between Alcohol and Bars & Night Clubs? People go to bars and clubs for numerous reasons. To get inebriated. To dance. To be with friends. To get away from a daily routine in their lives. A night out to relax, eat food and drink. To celebrate occasions. To attract and meet someone. Forget your problems. Or just to spend money. Whatever the reason, alcohol provides the sedative to lesson tensions and make the drinker less irritable. By removing inhibitions, it is suitable to make the drinker less shy and more talkative. This is why we find alcohol in a social atmosphere, because it works and makes money.

THE EFFECTS OF ALCOHOLIC BEVERAGES

When alcoholic beverages are consumed, the alcohol content is absorbed into the blood without digestion. A small percentage of the alcohol does not undergo chemical change but is eliminated from the body through breathing, urinating, or perspiring. Alcohol in the right quantity is sometimes used to stimulate food appetite and sex by stimulating the flow of saliva. Depending on the number of drinks consumed, alcohol can have one of two effects on an individual. The person can either develop a sense of euphoria or he may experience a feeling of depression. If alcohol beverages will be used, it should be consumed in moderation to prevent acute intoxication or complications. Excessive alcohol drinking is a habit forming drug which can lead to addiction, thus, developing serious health problems. Every possible precaution should be taken to help a patron of an establishment from becoming intoxicated to the point where his/her health or life of others is at risk. Instruct bartenders to stop serving individuals who they sense are intoxicated. Outline this in the employee's job duties and have him understand the liabilities. Ask a friend for a designated driver. Set up rides or lodgings if you feel it necessary. These are some of the ways you can protect yourself from a liability that may arise. The more you do and care for your patrons, the minimal your liabilities will be.

NIGHT CLUB STAFF AND OPERATING PROCEDURES

Your staff size should be calculated by the size of your establishment and the amount of your customers per open night.

Your staff should or may consist of the following:
Owners(s) / Manager(s) / Disc Jockey(s) / Bartender(s)
Bouncer(s) / Cashier(s) / Clean-up

Optional staff on call should or may consist of the following:
Valet Parking / Promoter(s) / Dancer(s) / Salesperson of Liquor Shots / Host or Hostess / Flower Person / Photographer / Light Controller for Dance Floor / Short Order Cook / Standby Limo / Restroom Attendant / MC Announcer

MEETINGS

Hold a short meeting with your staff before you open for the night. Advise your staff of your plans for the night. Tell your staff of what you expect from them as far as doing their jobs are concerned. All of your staff should always be courteous to the customers and treat them with respect. This rule particularly applies to your bouncers if you have them. Their size can intimidate some people so their personality has to make them feel welcome. If you serve food organize a good operation. Overall organize a respectable staff.

DISC JOCKEY

What does a "Disc Jockey" really do? Music is his life. He reports which records are hot and which are not to Record Pools, Tip Sheets, Magazines and others. He discovers which records are hot by dance floor responses in night clubs. Basically, he/she knows what works on the dance floor. If it's old or new, a DJ can possibly tell you who sings it and where you can find the, record. The DJ can make your crowd keep coming back for more of his music mixes. His music can sell, inspire, entertain, and attract crowds. Also his music can make people feel good, bring people together, create atmosphere, and recall memories of the past.

11

Because of the reputation of being the best DJ in the business, acquiring one or more of these DJ's on rotation increases an establishments chances of success.

SHOULD YOU CHARGE ADMISSION?

Eight basic guidelines why bars and night clubs may or may not charge door admission.

1) **Poor Economy** (Might have to charge to produce some type of income at door to stay in business.)

2) **Good Economy** (People have more spending money. People are going out more, it's up to you if you want to charge.)

3) **No Reason** (Your bar or club is happening. Customers not concerned about paying. They want to be there at all cost.)

4) **Live Radio Broadcast** (This is where it's happening. Radio is live and calling people to come down to location. It's fair to charge admission in most cases.)

5) **Special Events** (Singers, Bands or other events. Admission can be charged.)

6) **Top DJ** (People pay entrance to listen to this DJ. This is where the real party is.)

7) **Women.** (Wherever there is a lot of them or high class go go admission may be obtained.)

8) **Renovations.** (You've just completed them. You need to re-coop some of your investment. You may be able to charge admission.)

ADVERTISING

What is advertising? In a nutshell, "Untold is Unsold." Spreading the word about you is advertising. Some businesses might require more advertising than others. But just where should you advertise and how much? Is it wiser to spend more money on advertising in a poor economy than a good economy? Are you a new business?

If you are open, how is your business progressing at this very moment? Advertising, whether it's a large budget or small it is not a guaranteed ticket to increased business. But not advertising at all definitely means failure.

Promoters should understand that not one person likes to go to the same place everyday. Special events have a better chance of success than days with no events. That's one reason why promoters will have more than one club under their account.

The following is a true example of a night clubs poor management decisions:
An entrepreneur decides to open his night club in a location he thinks will do well. In his analysis, he determines it will be a sound investment and elects to proceed with his project. Within two square miles there are three other night clubs competing for the same customers. He spends close to $200,000 on his venture. His advertising budget for his "Grand Opening" was approximately $1,000. "The grand opening was a failure. Twenty people showed up at the three day weekend Grand Opening. In less than three weeks - he closed. His decisions were based by his own research and not asking for anyone's input. His advertising budget was too low for his investment. He did not want to spend advertising dollars for his grand opening that was to tell everyone you are open for business.

WHAT TYPES OF ADVERTISING ARE AVAILABLE?
1) Flyers / Most effective as postcard size. Can be used as a mailer. When distributed at the club, can easily be placed in a pocket or purse. Target distribution. Set up mailing lists. Basic size is 4"x 6". Smaller is also great for pockets and purses.

2) Invite Friends / Make those phone calls and invite your friends and their friends. Word of mouth travels fast if your having a special event. Place people on guest lists. Give complimentary drink passes. Get them in.

3) **Free Admission Passes & V.I.P's** / Print "Free" or "Reduced Admission" on some passes. Make use of V.I.P.'s.

4) **Radio and Television** / Radio and Cable Television are an effective means of reaching a large number of the population at a given time. Like other advertising, it should not be looked upon as guaranteed success. Check rates for best deals.

5) **Entertainment and Music Magazines** / People save and review magazines. Combined with other sources of advertising, it increases your circulation of exposure.

6) **Newspapers** / Excellent source of reaching large numbers of people. Drawbacks include not targeting a certain market and can at times become expensive.

7) **Special Exclusive Invitations by Mail** / Excellent source for requiring the presence of an individual for a special event.

8) **Promotional Materials** / Hats, shirts, key rings, jackets, lighters, imprinted balloons, pens, pencils, buttons, decals, drinking bar glasses, calendars, matches, etc.. Items are great for grand openings. There are approximately 10,000 different specialty items on the market which most can be imprinted with your name or message. Many are inexpensive enough to be given away.

9) **Promoter** / A good promoter can help you with the coordination of "Special Events" and distribution of promotional materials.

10) **Cd Music Handouts** / A different approach to promotions. Sample of the latest music can be recorded on a cd advertising your club dubbed over parts of the music. Check restrictions.

11) **Airplanes, Blimps, Weather Balloons** / If you are located

near the ocean, you may want to investigate these possibilities.

12) **Posters** / Make posters of certain scheduled events. Hang in bar or club, and different outdoor areas.

13) **Private Parties** / Rent your facility on off days to people or promoters who are looking for entertainment space. Contact possible clientele through mail announcing your facility for rent for their Christmas parties, Birthday parties, or other corporate parties.

14) **Billboards.** Highest traffic volume located on highway locations. Rates will vary.

WHAT SHOULD MY ADVERTISING DO?

An ad which is very well designed should be looked upon as more of an investment rather than an expense. A great ad will pay for itself in increased business so it really doesn't cost anything in the long run. Cut out, save, and compare ads and flyers of your competition. See what ideas might work for you. If you decide to buy an ad in any media, don't sign a long-term contract committing yourself until you've proved that the ad will work for you.

When advertising with flyers don't tell the entire story. Your copy should just get their attention and give the main message. Flyers need to be noticed. Use full color printing or fluorescent stock to attract more attention. Be aware of any additional costs involved for trimming, cutting, or printing of certain requests. "Your flyers must attract, Attention, Interest, Desire, and Action."

CONCLUSION

Remember that advertising should pay for itself. If it's not, it's not helping you. No matter how good the ad looks, it's worthless if it doesn't sell. A poor ad is worthless because you will not profit from it and will cost you money to produce and print. If an ad works, use it. If it doesn't, focus your efforts on different ways of getting noticed.

USING MAILING LISTS

An establishments mailing list objective is to inform potential customers of an upcoming event. Today, mailing lists prove to be an effective way of communicating. These mailing lists can be one of your company's most valuable assets. You can only expect a percentage of your mail out to work. Not everyone will be receptive of your offer. By acquiring this percentage you would of met your cost of mail and acquired your evening crowd.

Compiling and maintaining an effective mailing list requires that you first collect the information and then keep it accurate and up-to-date. Today, a term most widely used in collecting information about your consumer is called a "database." When you add or remove information from your database, you must develop ways of keeping your list clean by analyzing the   content. You will be accessing your list frequently. Your success in manipulating information quickly and efficiently will depend on how it is physically stored. There are also mailing houses who will   service and take care of all your mailing needs.

MAILING LIST STORAGE SYSTEM

There are many ways you are able to store your information. If you plan not to mail very often and have a small mailing you would probably be better off storing information on an index card system. This mailing list should be no more than two hundred names. Make use of your computer and self adhesive labels.

If you are planning to mail on a larger scale, you should implement a more efficient system. This system will include a computer with a software offering a variety of applications and functions.

There is a wide range of alternative software and mailing storage systems. Consult a computer specialist or related field and explain your business needs. One thing to remember, your selected package may also be able to perform functions other than your mailing list, such as; word processing, billing and budgeting. These packages help you spread the cost of the software into a number of areas.

LABEL INFORMATION

The following information needs to be included for each name on the list:

#1 A unique account number. The month & year of the acquired name can be utilized in the account number. Create a search condition on your software to easily locate this label for viewing, adding information or elimination.

#2 Name

#3 Street address or P.O. Box

#4 Apartment number, Suite number if supplied

#5 City

#6 State

#7 Zip Code, five or nine digits

DEVELOPING A MAILING LIST

"Prospects are potential customers." You have reason to believe they have a need or interest in your services. There are ways to separate information about your customers and therefore making different mailing lists. For example, you may be planning to promote a "Male Revue". You can create a "search condition" in your database and retrieve a listings of females only. You would feel that a woman mailing list would be your best choice for this event. Mailing lists can be divided in numerous ways: by age, income, automobiles, geographic location, etc..

EIGHT WAYS OF ACQUIRING A MAILING LIST

#1) Having employee(s) walking throughout the club asking if they would like to be placed on the mailing list. Very effective in developing a current mailing lists.

#2) Acquiring a list from another club who might be closing. Most likely, every night club has their own list.

#3) Acquiring a list from a promoter. His/her mailing list has been developed from club to club.

#4) Place information on your flyers reading: "How to be placed on the mailing list", with your address.

#5) Acquiring a list from a model, talent, booking agent. These mailing lists were developed of people who seeked the services of entertainment agencies at least one time or another. You might find this an excellent source.

#6) Review your phone book for mailing list companies. These companies offer a wide range of criteria to choose from and mailing labels are guaranteed deliverable or they will credit you.

#7) Develop your own mailing list through your Bar, Night Club Contest and VIP Forms."

#8) Record Pools Distributors. Names on these lists are primarily DJ's and promoters.

PROMOTIONAL IDEAS

The following are "Promotional Advertising Ideas" that have been demonstrated to be effective. Next to each idea you will find a brief explanation of its concept. It's up to the owner/promoter to further investigate and set up the concept in a way in which you can make your own adjustments to the idea. Following each idea is tracking. Indicate results achieved for future reference of event success should you wish to repeat the event.

#1) PRE-GRAND OPENING PARTY / Your bar or club has just opened for business. This party can be held during the week. Can be held for a couple of days. Most of this crowd is by invitation only. The concept is you have just finished construction on your club and this grand opening is a sneak preview for the special guests only. This party should include specials such as buffet, shirt giveaways, V.I.P. giveaways, free drink passes, drink specials, etc.

TRACKING:
Date of Event:_____ $ Generated from Event: _____
    - Expenses:_____   - Tax _____   Net Profit: _____
RESULTS: Successful ____   Moderate ____   Poor ____

#2) GRAND OPENING / This is your "Grand Opening Celebration" for the public. Should be held for 2 to 3 days. Everyone invited. Should include some type of entertainment and party atmosphere. VIP giveaways, free drink passes and possible buffet.

TRACKING:
Date of Event:_____ $ Generated from Event: _____
    - Expenses:_____   - Tax _____   Net Profit: _____
RESULTS: Successful ____   Moderate ____   Poor ____

#3) NEW YEARS EVE PARTY / Last day of December. Happy New Years! The most celebrated time in the world. Use your own ideas and concepts. Night clubs located in hotels offer discounts for room rentals. Possibilities of selling tickets 2 - 3 months in advance.

TRACKING:
Date of Event:_____ $ Generated from Event: _____
    - Expenses:_____   - Tax _____   Net Profit: _____
RESULTS: Successful ____   Moderate ____   Poor ____

Sergio Barone

#4) THE DAY AFTER NEW YEARS EVE PARTY / Your customers are still at your location. Offer coffee, pastries to your clientele. Price can be included in the New Years Eve party price.

TRACKING:
Date of Event:_____ $ Generated from Event: _____
- Expenses:_____ - Tax: _____ Net Profit: _____
RESULTS: Successful ____ Moderate ____ Poor ____

#5) VALENTINES DAY PARTY / February 14th. A christian festival commemorating the martyrdom of Saint Valentine on February 14, 270. Acceptance of Saint Valentine as patron saint of lovers appears to have been accidental. Medieval European belief that birds begin to mate on February 14th. This notion presumably suggested that lads and lasses should choose lovers and exchange gifts. Then the word "Valentine" was applied to both persons and presents. Have plenty of roses available for sale or giveaways at the door. Advertise drink specials (preferably a "red" color mixed drink), maybe call it a heartbreaker, use your imagination.

TRACKING:
Date of Event:_____ $ Generated from Event: _____
- Expenses:_____ - Tax: _____ Net Profit: _____
RESULTS: Successful ____ Moderate ____ Poor ____

#6) ST. PATRICK'S DAY PARTY / March 17th. Think "Green." Possible ideas: Offer free admission or a drink to anyone wearing green. Offer buffet.

TRACKING:
Date of Event:_____ $ Generated from Event: _____
- Expenses:_____ - Tax: _____ Net Profit: _____
RESULTS: Successful ____ Moderate ____ Poor ____

#7) BEGINNING OF SPRING PARTY / March 20th. Possibilities: Advertise free admission to ladies with skirts. Have an overall party atmosphere. Beer on tap. Entertainment. Shirts, hats, etc.. Possible Live Radio Broadcast.

TRACKING:
Date of Event:_____ $ Generated from Event: _____
- Expenses:_____ - Tax: _____ Net Profit: _____
RESULTS: Successful ____ Moderate ____ Poor ____

20

#8) EASTER EGG HUNT / Purchase empty plastic eggs from a crafts store. Stuff with coupon redeemable for money or prize. Advertise one egg containing a large prize of money. Hide them in your bar or club.

TRACKING:
Date of Event:_____ $ Generated from Event: _____
  - Expenses:_____   - Tax _____   Net Profit: _____
RESULTS: Successful ____   Moderate ____   Poor ____

#9) MEMORIAL DAY WEEKEND PARTY / March 20th. You are able to utilize 3 days for this event. Possible radio broadcast. Party atmosphere. One of the largest celebrations of the year. Bikini contests.

TRACKING:
Date of Event:_____ $ Generated from Event: _____
  - Expenses:_____   - Tax _____   Net Profit: _____
RESULTS: Successful ____   Moderate ____   Poor ____

#10) SUMMER PARTY/ June 21st. This is the beginning of the summer. Make use of items which remind you of summer. Possibilities: Bikini Contests, Singers, Live Radio Broadcasts, Best Body Contest, etc.. Utilize throughout the summer. Drink specials, giveaways, T-shirts, sunglasses. Good time for sponsorships.

TRACKING:
Date of Event:_____ $ Generated from Event: _____
  - Expenses:_____   - Tax _____   Net Profit: _____
RESULTS: Successful ____   Moderate ____   Poor ____

#11) FOURTH OF JULY PARTY / July 4th. "Independence Day." One of the chief legal holidays of the United States, commemorates the formal adoption of the Declaration of Independence. It's a celebration of barbecues and fireworks. Run beer specials. If you are planning a large party submit your ideas for sponsorship from beer companies.

TRACKING:
Date of Event:_____ $ Generated from Event: _____
  - Expenses:_____   - Tax _____   Net Profit: _____
RESULTS: Successful ____   Moderate ____   Poor ____

21

#12) LABOR DAY WEEKEND / September 2nd. In the United States and Canada, a holiday observed on the first Monday in September. You are able to utilize three days for parties. Marking the near of the end of summer. Use party atmosphere. Possibilities: live radio broadcast, drink specials, etc.

TRACKING:

Date of Event:_____ $ Generated from Event: _____

 - Expenses:_____ - Tax _____   Net Profit: _____

RESULTS: Successful ____ Moderate ____ Poor ____

#13) END OF SUMMER PARTY / September 23. This is when "Autumn" begins.

TRACKING:

Date of Event:_____ $ Generated from Event: _____

 - Expenses:_____ - Tax _____   Net Profit: _____

RESULTS: Successful ____ Moderate ____ Poor ____

#14) HALLOWEEN PARTY / October 31st. Best days to have your party are the days before and after Halloween or both. Everyone else is having it on Halloween and you would be in competition with everyone. Costumes are usually rented for 3 days if not purchased. One of the largest and successful parties of the year. Hold costume contests. Offer prizes.

TRACKING:

Date of Event:_____ $ Generated from Event: _____

 - Expenses:_____ - Tax _____   Net Profit: _____

RESULTS: Successful ____ Moderate ____ Poor ____

#15) THANKSGIVING PARTY / November 28th. No work the next day. One of the biggest parties of the year.

TRACKING:

Date of Event:_____ $ Generated from Event: _____

 - Expenses:_____ - Tax _____   Net Profit: _____

RESULTS: Successful ____ Moderate ____ Poor ____

#16) CHRISTMAS PARTY/ December 25th. Usually held the weekend before Christmas. Offer buffet and drinks on the house for a couple of hours or more.

TRACKING:

Date of Event:_____ $ Generated from Event: _____

  - Expenses:_____   - Tax _____   Net Profit: _____

RESULTS: Successful ____   Moderate ____   Poor ____

#17) YOUR BARS, NIGHT CLUB'S ANNIVERSARY PARTY Celebrate your club's anniversary. Hold different types of specials and entertainment.

TRACKING:

Date of Event:_____ $ Generated from Event: _____

  - Expenses:_____   - Tax _____   Net Profit: _____

RESULTS: Successful ____   Moderate ____   Poor ____

#18) BIRTHDAY PARTIES / Celebrate owners, employees, promoters, dj's, etc..

TRACKING:

Date of Event:_____ $ Generated from Event: _____

  - Expenses:_____   - Tax _____   Net Profit: _____

RESULTS: Successful ____   Moderate ____   Poor ____

#19) FRIDAY, SATURDAY NIGHT DANCE PARTY / Possible broadcast live on the radio from your establishment. Promote popular acts.

TRACKING:

Date of Event:_____ $ Generated from Event: _____

  - Expenses:_____   - Tax _____   Net Profit: _____

RESULTS: Successful ____   Moderate ____   Poor ____

#20) LADIES NIGHT / Build one day a week catering to women. Free admission, reduced drink prices, male revues, champagne cocktails, etc..

TRACKING:

Date of Event:_____ $ Generated from Event: _____

  - Expenses:_____   - Tax _____   Net Profit: _____

RESULTS: Successful ____   Moderate ____   Poor ____

#21) FEMALE, MALE REVUE / Seek the services of different performers and companies. Check city ordinances for restrictions.
TRACKING:
Date of Event:_____ $ Generated from Event: _____
  - Expenses:_____ - Tax _____   Net Profit: _____
RESULTS: Successful ____   Moderate ____   Poor ____

#22) TEEN YOUNG ADULT NIGHT / Offer night(s) to the teen crowd. (No Alcohol) Check local ordinances for restrictions. Have popular entertainers perform.
TRACKING:
Date of Event:_____ $ Generated from Event: _____
  - Expenses:_____ - Tax _____   Net Profit: _____
RESULTS: Successful ____   Moderate ____   Poor ____

#23) BEACH PARTY / Create a beach atmosphere. Offer drink specials such as "Sex on the Beach". Possible bikini contests.
TRACKING:
Date of Event:_____ $ Generated from Event: _____
  - Expenses:_____ - Tax _____   Net Profit: _____
RESULTS: Successful ____   Moderate ____   Poor ____

#24) SUPER JAM CONCERT / Seek promoter who can acquire top name singers / performers to appear for a one night large event.
TRACKING:
Date of Event:_____ $ Generated from Event: _____
  - Expenses:_____ - Tax _____   Net Profit: _____
RESULTS: Successful ____   Moderate ____   Poor ____

#25) MUSIC AWARDS / Seek promoter who can organize this type of event for your facility. Best artist, song, etc. Create categories.
TRACKING:
Date of Event:_____ $ Generated from Event: _____
  - Expenses:_____ - Tax _____   Net Profit: _____
RESULTS: Successful ____   Moderate ____   Poor ____

#26) RECORD RELEASE PARTY / Seek promoter who can set up this party for a artist that's releasing a new song.
TRACKING:
Date of Event:_____ $ Generated from Event: _____
  - Expenses:_____ - Tax _____   Net Profit: _____
RESULTS: Successful ____ Moderate ___ Poor ___

#27) BIKINI CONTEST / Seek the services of a promoter who can organize such an event.
TRACKING:
Date of Event:_____ $ Generated from Event: _____
  - Expenses:_____ - Tax _____   Net Profit: _____
RESULTS: Successful ____ Moderate ___ Poor ___

#28) FASHION SHOW / Seek the services of a promoter who can organize such an event.
TRACKING:
Date of Event:_____ $ Generated from Event: _____
  - Expenses:_____ - Tax _____   Net Profit: _____
RESULTS: Successful ____ Moderate ___ Poor ___

#29) HOT BODIES CONTEST / Organize a contest for best looking bodies. Have judges pick the best looking bods to win.
TRACKING:
Date of Event:_____ $ Generated from Event: _____
  - Expenses:_____ - Tax _____   Net Profit: _____
RESULTS: Successful ____ Moderate ___ Poor ___

#30) MODELING CASTING CONTRACT / Seek promoter who can arrange this event. Winner of contest is offered modeling contract by known agency. Set up contest with agency.
TRACKING:
Date of Event:_____ $ Generated from Event: _____
  - Expenses:_____ - Tax _____   Net Profit: _____
RESULTS: Successful ____ Moderate ___ Poor ___

#31) V.I.P. Party / Make arrangements to invite all friends and business associates and all VIP card holders to a one day special VIP event. Offer food and entertainment.

TRACKING:
Date of Event:_____ $ Generated from Event: _____
  - Expenses:_____ - Tax _____   Net Profit: _____
RESULTS: Successful ____ Moderate ____ Poor ____

#32) STAFF NIGHT / Offer drinks and buffet to staff and invited guests.

TRACKING:
Date of Event:_____ $ Generated from Event: _____
  - Expenses:_____ - Tax _____   Net Profit: _____
RESULTS: Successful ____ Moderate ____ Poor ____

#33) DJ COLLABORATION PARTY / Setup a number of DJ's to attend and dj at your club.

TRACKING:
Date of Event:_____ $ Generated from Event: _____
  - Expenses:_____ - Tax _____   Net Profit: _____
RESULTS: Successful ____ Moderate ____ Poor ____

#34) RAFFLES / Offer a free weekly raffle to win a super prize at the end of a set amount of weeks or months.

TRACKING:
Date of Event:_____ $ Generated from Event: _____
  - Expenses:_____ - Tax _____   Net Profit: _____
RESULTS: Successful ____ Moderate ____ Poor ____

#35) HOUSE PARTY / Just another term for a party at your club. Use plenty of balloons and decorative items. Possible buffet.

TRACKING:
Date of Event:_____ $ Generated from Event: _____
  - Expenses:_____ - Tax _____   Net Profit: _____
RESULTS: Successful ____ Moderate ____ Poor ____

#36) NUTS & BOLTS / Locate where you can obtain different types of threaded nuts and bolts. Give women the nuts and give men the bolts. Let them locate the matching threads to win a trip. Nuts & bolts can also be all threaded correctly, but color coded with paint to make a matching set. Call out for the couple with matching nuts and bolts. Object is for the ladies and gentlemen to meet. Offer drinks, dinner or prizes to the lucky winners.

TRACKING:
Date of Event:_____ $ Generated from Event: _____

  - Expenses:_____   - Tax: _____   Net Profit: _____

RESULTS: Successful ____   Moderate ____   Poor ____

#37) DRINK OR PENNY 'TILL U PEE / Charge admission such as $4.99, give back 1 cent to customer. Customers purchase drinks for 1 cent until someone has to use the restroom. Once someone uses the restroom or wants to exit premise prices resume to normal. Point out the person to the crowd who had to use the restroom. Have bouncers on hand near restroom for angry crowd.

TRACKING:
Date of Event:_____ $ Generated from Event: _____

  - Expenses:_____   - Tax: _____   Net Profit: _____

RESULTS: Successful ____   Moderate ____   Poor ____

#38) SUPERBOWL SUNDAY / Make use of all your television monitors for the superbowl. Offer some type of drinks and buffet for a cover charge. Also may apply to other favorite sporting events.

TRACKING:
Date of Event:_____ $ Generated from Event: _____

  - Expenses:_____   - Tax: _____   Net Profit: _____

RESULTS: Successful ____   Moderate ____   Poor ____

#39) MAGAZINE PARTY / Contact different music, bar magazines who look to promote their parties.

TRACKING:
Date of Event:_____ $ Generated from Event: _____

  - Expenses:_____   - Tax: _____   Net Profit: _____

RESULTS: Successful ____   Moderate ____   Poor ____

Sergio Barone

#40) WELCOME BACK FROM VACATIONS PARTY/ Concept welcomes customers back from their vacations. Ideal time for use is September.
TRACKING:
Date of Event:_____ $ Generated from Event: _____
  - Expenses:_____ - Tax _____   Net Profit: _____
RESULTS: Successful ____ Moderate ____ Poor ____

#41) DANCE CONTEST / Promoter organizes dance contest. Award prizes for singles or couples. Contestants bring their own music.
TRACKING:
Date of Event:_____ $ Generated from Event: _____
  - Expenses:_____ - Tax _____   Net Profit: _____
RESULTS: Successful ____ Moderate ____ Poor ____

#42) TROPICAL LUAU / Offer free t-shirts and gifts to be given away. Create an island atmosphere with props. Offer tropical drinks. Offer different tropical island captions. Possibility: Offer Tropical Island trip giveaway after 4 weeks.
TRACKING:
Date of Event:_____ $ Generated from Event: _____
  - Expenses:_____ - Tax _____   Net Profit: _____
RESULTS: Successful ____ Moderate ____ Poor ____

#43) SINGLES PARTY / Find a dating service who specializes in these types of parties.
TRACKING:
Date of Event:_____ $ Generated from Event: _____
  - Expenses:_____ - Tax _____   Net Profit: _____
RESULTS: Successful ____ Moderate ____ Poor ____

#44) RECORD CONVENTION / Contact retail record outlets to set up tables at your facility. Object is for retailers to offer hard to find records. Promote special guest appearances and acts.
TRACKING:
Date of Event:_____ $ Generated from Event: _____
  - Expenses:_____ - Tax _____   Net Profit: _____
RESULTS: Successful ____ Moderate ____ Poor ____

28

#45) CONCERT SERIES / If you have a large capacity indoor or outdoor facility, you can promote a series of concerts attracting big name acts.

TRACKING:
Date of Event:_____ $ Generated from Event: _____
- Expenses:_____   - Tax _____   Net Profit: _____
RESULTS: Successful ____   Moderate ____   Poor ____

#46) RECORD POOL DISTRIBUTORS PARTY / Record pools hold their monthly parties and meeting at bars & night clubs. They almost always provide entertainment.

TRACKING:
Date of Event:_____ $ Generated from Event: _____
- Expenses:_____   - Tax _____   Net Profit: _____
RESULTS: Successful ____   Moderate ____   Poor ____

#47) HAPPY HOUR / Offer reduced drink specials, no admission, buffet.

TRACKING:
Date of Event:_____ $ Generated from Event: _____
- Expenses:_____   - Tax _____   Net Profit: _____
RESULTS: Successful ____   Moderate ____   Poor ____

#48) WILD WEDNESDAYS / Anything goes type of atmosphere. Have fast talking Emcees. Offer raffles, etc.

TRACKING:
Date of Event:_____ $ Generated from Event: _____
- Expenses:_____   - Tax _____   Net Profit: _____
RESULTS: Successful ____   Moderate ____   Poor ____

#49) THIRSTY THURSDAYS / Offer drink specials, every hour on the hour.

TRACKING:
Date of Event:_____ $ Generated from Event: _____
- Expenses:_____   - Tax _____   Net Profit: _____
RESULTS: Successful ____   Moderate ____   Poor ____

#50) HOT & HORNY / Print cards with the word "Horny" with a different number on all cards. Distribute to the gentlemen. Print cards with the word "Hot" for the ladies with matching numbers for the cards "Horny. Distribute at the entrance. Call out the numbers and look for that couple. Object is for ladies and the gentlemen to meet. You can offer drinks or dinner to the lucky winners.

TRACKING:

Date of Event:_____ $ Generated from Event: _____

   - Expenses:_____   - Tax _____   Net Profit _____

RESULTS: Successful ____   Moderate ____   Poor ____

#51) BEAT THE CLOCK / Charge regular admission. Start at 9:00pm offering tap beers at .50 cents. Then every half hour raise price of beer .50 cents until you reach your regular price at end of night. Object is to have customers arrive early to take advantage of specially announced beer drink prices.

TRACKING:

Date of Event:_____ $ Generated from Event: _____

   - Expenses:_____   - Tax _____   Net Profit _____

RESULTS: Successful ____   Moderate ____   Poor ____

#52) THE VELCRO WALL / Customers come in to try the "Velcro Wall". The object of the velcro wall is for a person to change into a velcro suit, take a small run, jump onto a trampoline and head for the wall. Result is person gets stuck on the wall. Person who gets stuck the highest receives free shots or some type of prize. Contact proper promoter for this event.

TRACKING:

Date of Event:_____ $ Generated from Event: _____

   - Expenses:_____   - Tax _____   Net Profit _____

RESULTS: Successful ____   Moderate ____   Poor ____

#53) BODY SHOTS / Set up area near bar where patrons pay for mixed drink or shot. Bartender pours liquor down their throats.

TRACKING:

Date of Event:_____ $ Generated from Event: _____

   - Expenses:_____   - Tax _____   Net Profit _____

RESULTS: Successful ____   Moderate ____   Poor ____

#54) CABLE T.V. / Contact cable t.v. to video your club and air on cable station as a dance party channel.

TRACKING:

Date of Event:_____ $ Generated from Event: _____

    - Expenses:_____ - Tax _____   Net Profit: _____

RESULTS: Successful ____   Moderate ____   Poor ____

#55) SUNDAY NITE JAM / Create a party atmosphere on this usually slow night.

TRACKING:

Date of Event:_____ $ Generated from Event: _____

    - Expenses:_____ - Tax _____   Net Profit: _____

RESULTS: Successful ____   Moderate ____   Poor ____

#56) MUSCLE CONTEST / Get in touch with health clubs to compete in a muscle contest. Hold finals. Health clubs offer reduced rate memberships.

TRACKING:

Date of Event:_____ $ Generated from Event: _____

    - Expenses:_____ - Tax _____   Net Profit: _____

RESULTS: Successful ____   Moderate ____   Poor ____

#57) COLLEGE NIGHT / Play music that colleges listen to. Advertise it as their night. Contact colleges to let them know that your facility is available for their parties.

TRACKING:

Date of Event:_____ $ Generated from Event: _____

    - Expenses:_____ - Tax _____   Net Profit: _____

RESULTS: Successful ____   Moderate ____   Poor ____

#58) $25.00 EVERY HOUR ON THE HOUR / Offer a money giveaway to customers. Choose by raffle a winner every hour of $25.00 Chances are winning customers will spend back into the bar and keep coming back for more.

TRACKING:

Date of Event:_____ $ Generated from Event: _____

    - Expenses:_____ - Tax _____   Net Profit: _____

RESULTS: Successful ____   Moderate ____   Poor ____

31

#59) THE FINAL DAYS / If your establishment is about to close its doors and join the clubituaries, you can advertise it in that way. People will go to the last days of a night club. Possibilities exist when you reopen under a different name.

TRACKING:

Date of Event:_____ $ Generated from Event: _____

 - Expenses:_____   - Tax _____   Net Profit: _____

RESULTS: Successful ____   Moderate ____   Poor ____

#60) BUNS CONTEST / Promoter organizes a buns contest. Specify for female or male participants. Give prizes or have finals for the winners.

TRACKING:

Date of Event:_____ $ Generated from Event: _____

 - Expenses:_____   - Tax _____   Net Profit: _____

RESULTS: Successful ____   Moderate ____   Poor ____

#61) NATIONALITY NIGHT / Cater to different Clientele. Example: Latin Night, Italian Night, etc.

TRACKING:

Date of Event:_____ $ Generated from Event: _____

 - Expenses:_____   - Tax _____   Net Profit: _____

RESULTS: Successful ____   Moderate ____   Poor ____

#62) WET T-SHIRT CONTEST / Preferably for the summer. Promoter organizes a bikini contest with a twist of water. Hold finals. Give prizes.

TRACKING:

Date of Event:_____ $ Generated from Event: _____

 - Expenses:_____   - Tax _____   Net Profit: _____

RESULTS: Successful ____   Moderate ____   Poor ____

#63) DJ SPIN OFF CONTEST / Battle of the DJ's. Invite DJ's to compete against each other for different titles. Set systems up on stage. Hold finals.

TRACKING:

Date of Event:_____ $ Generated from Event: _____

 - Expenses:_____   - Tax _____   Net Profit: _____

RESULTS: Successful ____   Moderate ____   Poor ____

#64) T-SHIRT GIVEAWAY NIGHT / Good for promoting something new at your club. Some customers receive a shirt ticket at the door to claim a free t-shirt. T-shirt has your business name imprinted with a caption.

TRACKING:

Date of Event:_____ $ Generated from Event: _____

- Expenses:_____ - Tax: _____   Net Profit: _____

RESULTS: Successful ____ Moderate ____ Poor ____

#65) KARAOKE / People take turns singing along to the backgrounds of their favorite songs. Offer prizes to ultimate winner.

TRACKING:

Date of Event:_____ $ Generated from Event: _____

- Expenses:_____ - Tax _____   Net Profit: _____

RESULTS: Successful ____ Moderate ____ Poor ____

#66) THE DATING GAME / Popularized by the "Dating Game" on television. You can use the same concept.

TRACKING:

Date of Event:_____ $ Generated from Event: _____

- Expenses:_____ - Tax _____   Net Profit: _____

RESULTS: Successful ____ Moderate ____ Poor ____

#67) BAND NIGHT / Have a popular band perform at your establishment.

TRACKING:

Date of Event:_____ $ Generated from Event: _____

- Expenses:_____ - Tax _____   Net Profit: _____

RESULTS: Successful ____ Moderate ____ Poor ____

#68) BATTLE OF THE BANDS / Have bands sign up to compete against each other weekly.

TRACKING:

Date of Event:_____ $ Generated from Event: _____

- Expenses:_____ - Tax _____   Net Profit: _____

RESULTS: Successful ____ Moderate ____ Poor ____

#69) TRACK ACTS / Music Artist's sing to their pre-recorded background music.

TRACKING:

Date of Event:_____ $ Generated from Event: _____

- Expenses:_____ - Tax _____ Net Profit _____

RESULTS: Successful ____ Moderate ____ Poor ____

#70) MUSIC NITES / Advertise different types of music for each night. Example: Dance Music Night, Rock Night, Reggae Night, etc.

TRACKING:

Date of Event:_____ $ Generated from Event: _____

- Expenses:_____ - Tax _____ Net Profit _____

RESULTS: Successful ____ Moderate ____ Poor ____

#71) GOING TO GO GO NIGHT / For one night turn your bar or night club into a go go bar. Check any city restrictions.

TRACKING:

Date of Event:_____ $ Generated from Event: _____

- Expenses:_____ - Tax _____ Net Profit _____

RESULTS: Successful ____ Moderate ____ Poor ____

#72) COMEDIAN NITE / Stage a contest for locals for comedian nite. Offer prizes. Hire Promoter if necessary.

TRACKING:

Date of Event:_____ $ Generated from Event: _____

- Expenses:_____ - Tax _____ Net Profit _____

RESULTS: Successful ____ Moderate ____ Poor ____

#73) ALTERNATIVE LIFESTYLE NIGHTS / You may be able to create one or more nights catering to gay/lesbian crowd. Drawback is you may be known as this type of establishment in the future. Ok if that's your goal.

TRACKING:

Date of Event:_____ $ Generated from Event: _____

- Expenses:_____ - Tax _____ Net Profit _____

RESULTS: Successful ____ Moderate ____ Poor ____

#74) RAVE CLUB / One of the fastest growing trends in the country. Party goers dance to trance, trip hop, etc. music. Depending on the scale of your set-up rave nights on the average are getting $10 to $100 admission per person.

TRACKING:

Date of Event:_____ $ Generated from Event: _____

- Expenses:_____   - Tax: _____   Net Profit: _____

RESULTS: Successful ____   Moderate ____   Poor ____

#75) FOAM PARTY / Someone shoots foam from a foam cannon into a crowded dancefloor. Crowd swimming through foam. Popularized in other countries.

TRACKING:

Date of Event:_____ $ Generated from Event: _____

- Expenses:_____   - Tax: _____   Net Profit: _____

RESULTS: Successful ____   Moderate ____   Poor ____

Establishment terms as defined by Websters Dictionary.

Bar - A counter or place where liquor is served to customers.

Barroom - A place devoted exclusively to the serving of alcoholic beverages; a bar, taproom, tavern.

Night Club - A cafe' or restaurant serving liquor and food and presenting entertainment from night until early morning.

Discotheque - A small informal night club popularized in the United States in the 1960's, where the patrons dance to recorded music.

Cafe' - A coffeehouse; a restaurant; a barroom, tavern, or night club; coffee.

Pub - A public house; tavern.

Inn - A public house for the lodging and entertainment of travelers; a small hotel or restaurant; a tavern.

Lounge - A room open to the public where liquor is served, as in a hotel.

Saloon - A bar, taproom or tavern, a large public room or place used for one particular purpose; a secluded area of a bar which is lavishly furnished and reserved for those of high social status.

Taproom - A room where beer is served from the tap; a common room for drinking in a tavern; a cocktail lounge; a barroom.

Tavern - A place where alcoholic beverages are sold by the drink, an inn.

Theater - Dramatic representation as a division of the performing arts; dramatic quality or impact; as, wonderful theater; the locality where important events take place.

About the Author

Sergio Barone began promoting entertainment with his friends when he was barely of legal drinking age. He drew his first flyer by hand and rented a hall promoting free beer with door admission. His first party attracted nearly 250 people. Soon he was promoting 1 hall party per month. Gradually he started promoting bars and night clubs. He would arrange name singers to appear at night clubs every week. He also developed some promotional ideas that have been used in the NY   tri-state area. He then began developing industry start-up music magazines. Having made contacts throughout the industry in the 1980's and 90's, today he designs, markets and advertises for a variety of businesses.